Hypnosis

and

Pain Management

The study of the Hypno-Analgesia Process

Volume 1

Christophe Pank

Table des matières

Introduction

Nowadays in the hypnosis world, we are lucky to have more and more communication with the extensive media.

We can witness an **interest of the general medicine** arousing towards this marvellous subject when, and for years, le medical world never ceased to deny the use of this method.

In my genre, The **Elmanian Hypnosis**, The **'medical' hypnosis** has always been present in the practitioners' minds.

Dave Elman, who wasn't a doctor, had a very particular status in this domain as he was **a pain management specialist,** an analgesia and anesthesia specialist.

He was partnering with dentists and surgeons during their interventions. Hypnosis, as a pain management tool, is one of the first goals to the Elmanian Hypnosis.

Today in France, many patients ('Partners' in my semantic) are looking for practitioners to alleviate their pain, may they be acute or chronic. This essay has the set objective to **propose exercices and techniques** as much for practitioners as for partners.

I am not a doctor neither a pain specialist, so, what is offered in this book is an experience return and an overview of techniques and principles which can open doors in pain management.

It is however essential to consult **doctors when pain occurs**. Pain is an alarm and to 'take it away' would be like ignoring an alarm in a jewellers

More than to 'believe' in this or that, I would advise you to try it. You will then see for yourself that the **possibilities are closer than you would think.**

Chapter 1 : Is Hypnosis magical ?

For Partners :

Hypnosis is not magical. It is a field which uses a **natural state** called **trance**. Trance happens **daily** in all of us. It is the link between the conscious and the subconscious. In an easier way, between our **logical thinking and our imagination**.

It is important to keep in mind these two points : it is natural and daily. It is because you live this particular state regularly that the practitioner can make you 'relive'it.

To be specific :

- Did you ever gaze into space ? Thinking of something else while someone is talking to you, hence lose track of the conversation ?
- Did you ever feel completely off track but automatically do what it was you needed to do ?
- Did you ever experience strong emotions whilst reading a book or watching a movie ?
- Have you ever thought that your spouse talked to you when really he/she didn't ?

Well, all these examples are **trances**. Daily trances which we **live since we were born**.

This is why Hypnosis is no magic, this method uses and exploits its maximum, this facet of yourself.

Maybe **you just didn't call it being in a trance**, but instead : to be west, out of touch, shy-high, to lack attention, to be distracted…These are all trances.

It is though what, us practitioners under hypnosis, **would technically call** trances, and that is what we use to help phsychologically and physically our partners. That is what our friends of Hypnosis on stage use aswell for their shows with things that seem completely crazy.

As you can see, from this **very simple sensation** to be gazing and being elsewhere, there are tremendous opportunities to direct this situation **towards more incredible things**.

Now the immediate question popping into your mind : I live trances, yes, but I can't enter into a state of catalepsy, to hallucinate or to feel what I want to ?

And that is perfectly normal, how could you run a 400 metres **if you do not know how to run, jump, or last 400 metres** ? Or go for the 24 Hours of Le Mans when you never have driven a race car ? Neither attempted an endurance race ?

However, you know how to walk and run, in your own way, since you were a child. **Every possibility start with a first step,** to be aware of your trances is a first step.

About the pain, you have, since childhood, **this capacity to diminish, even to remove** it and for several minutes or even hours.

Think of the 'kissing better' from your mother, which succeeded to make disappear tears and pains that were caused by scratching or a sprained ankle.

The number of times that you bumped into a wall and that the pain disappeared after a few hours because **your spirit was busy with some more important tasks**. Tooth or stomach pains disappearing in front of other more important events.

I remember this partner who just a few minutes before arriving to my office almost had an accident. She was so stressed that her tooth pain **was gone** though this had been almost unbearable during the past few days. It is one of the **most extraordinary ways in which we function**. We can remove pain. And the tool we will use for this is trance and all its possibilities.

For practitioners :

We all know that our use of the pain management is natural. We also know, as mentioned in previous examples, that we can work through this **dissociative capacity which many have naturally**. Let's keep in mind that we all are different.

Some partners are not going to feel any pain and realise the hurt only later at home when they see the bruise…some others will on the other hand have an **associative quality.**

In this case, we need to play with this facet of the being and create a link **as an anchor**. You know the principles of **anchor's desactivation** with the creation of a new resource, you just need to do a similar process :

- Take **the pain as an anchor** and reflect in it all negative effects
- Work in **submodality** in order to diminish the information of pain
- Put in place a resource area, completely neutral, on another part of the body.
- As you **dissociate the area of pain, you associate resources** in the new anchor's partner.

We have to stay in an observational approach of our partner and be aware of how trance is working.

It is the exploitation of the trance associated/dissociated, opened/closed, that we will be able to offer a strategy and suggestions towards a possible diminishing of the pain.

Chapter 2 : What can hypnosis do against pain ?

As said before, I am neither a doctor nor a pain specialist. I will offer to work on **two types of pain.**

- **Acute pains** which are well known for their **short duration** and **following a precise cause.** They disappear when the cause **is healed**, for example, a cut.
- Chronic pains which last **at least 3 months and carry on** even with treatment and even if the cause is healed.

With hypnosis, we are going to be able to work on both through diverse ways and tools.

We need to keep in mind that pain is an important **information** in our life. If we didn't feel pain, we would put ourselves in **vital danger** constantly, to be sure of this, we just need to take a look at the congenital insensitivity illness. To give you an example, one of my friends who handles very well her trances, asked me **an anchor**, which is some kind of **activation button** that she can manage a pain which was recurrent in her life. She succeeded very quickly to resolve her issue and pains **were disappearing as soon as** her anchor was activated. One day, whilst working, she sprained her ankle which was pretty disabling.

She used her anchor to diminish her pain until **she forgot about it**. We surely could rejoice about this and think that it would be great if we could do the same. One thing though is that when she came back home in the evening, her ankle was **extremely swollen** and she was very close to having a **ruptured** ligament. We know that any pain tells you about a **physical malfunction**, and more subtly, and especially if the pain doesn't go away, about a **psychic malfunction**.

When you experience pain and before trying to do any of the tools offered in this essay, **go and see a doctor**. Some pains can be symptoms of other things.

There are different possibilities with hypnosis. As practitioners, we always try to **ease as much pain as possible**, and moreover, to return the partner to their **independance**. We do not want to become medicine for the ones who suffer from pain. Firstly, because we are expensive and we are not reimbursed by the social security, and secondly because we firmly believe that **partners are masters of their lives and bodies.**

Hypnosis is a natural tool, as I explained previously, therefore we want to offer you teachings as to how to use this capacity which is yours.

You can find different practitioners **depending on the activities** they offer.

In a practice, you will be able to work on both types of pain and act on it. You will be able to understand the 'symbolic' origin of this information.

In the medical world, you are now able to have surgery whilst under hypnosis. This application is more and more famous and used, and as I said before, it is not new. In the 50's already, this application was proven. To go further, **before the discovery of the chloroform** in 1845, James Braid was performing amputations under hypnosis and in a trance level (we will come back to this concept later) which Dave Elman called Hypnotic Coma.

In a time like this where most surgeries ended in death, he was succeeding to operate with his **patients, who were unable to feel any pain**. You can easily imagine that today, with all the progress of modern medicine techniques and practitioners, it is entirely secure to operate under hypnosis.

In Europe, this return to hypnosis is due to **Dr De Faymonville** who offered in the first place the sedation-hypnosis which is to use **a little bit of anesthetic** and work under hypnosis. At any sign of discomfort, there was a possibility to put the patient asleep.

There is a **fundamental difference** to note between medical staff (doctors, nurses…) and hypnosis practitioners in practice.

These latter **can't go with you in the operating theatre** (though some private clinics authorise them), **they cannot diagnose and are not doctors substitutes.**

They can help greatly in the management of acute and chronic pain.

Chapter 3 : How does it work ?

It is the part where things get a little more sharp, and which for who want to only learn the techniques can be passed over. Even if I try to simplify at its maximum hypnosis principles, it is possible that it may still be a little complex.

In the science of Hypnosis, we adopt a quite **specific scheme** as a pattern of the pshyche. This perception is typical for this genre and does not pretend to be the absolute truth.

If you want more explanations about Hard Sciences, you need to look closer in Neuro-Sciences. Psyche is a **soft science with more theories than 'truths'**. For example, the description of the Psyche by Freud is different from Berne's and both explanations don't **hinder a therapeutic well-being**.

We are going to see a few elements :

- **Conscious :** Short term memory, logical facets and analytical facets
- **Subconscious :** Emotions, long term memory, pattern, beliefs and values
- **Unconscious :** Whole automotised system of the body, sympathetic nervous system and parasympathetic

- **Administration Sas (Critic Analysis)** : System found between the conscious and the subconscious and then another one between the unconscious and the subconscious. They validate, invalidate or keep the information.

The goal is to make **the conscious communicate with the subconscious** the more 'directly'possible so that **the information goes** to the unconscious. As we are going to have to go through the **two administration sas**, acting like two customs administration points, it is interesting to make the communication happen at **a certain level of trance**.

Trance is the **communication** between the conscious, the subconscious and the unconscious, allowing (in a figure of speech) not to have to show your passport each time. There are levels of trance, as there are levels of accreditations, which permit to channel more or less information so that it can become a **suggestion, then a physiological appeasement**. We are going to work on the trances which let the suggestion become a **physical answer**.

Either in Hetero-hypnosis, meaning accompanied by a practitioner, or in Self-hypnosis, meaning **without any external intervention**, the process will be the same.

As indicated earlier, trances are natural, we have the capacity to analgesise ourselves. **Even more incredible,** the subconscious which **registered all memories** in the long term, is going to **'remember'** all memories of anesthesia received naturally or chemically.

It is one of the strengths of hypnosis to recall to the body this particular chemical capacity lived before and **to reuse it in a therapeutic approach…without the side effects**. We are very rarely anesthetising, but rather analgising.

It is important to keep this in mind during your experiences. You are going to feel if you are pinched or bitten but **no pain will be added**.

When we make a demonstration of a few minutes, yes, in 2-3 minutes, **we can diminish or even take away entirely the sensation of pain and very quickly**, and that we ask to our partner if all is ok when we pinch him/her…he/she systematically answers that he/she can **feel the pinch…but not the pain**. So, do not expect the same result than an anesthetic like in a hospital or at a dentists.

We can go to these deep levels called H-Ultra, I will talk about it in another part of the book, this technique will be for practitioners, it is not advised for beginners in self-hypnosis.

Now, let's get down to business.

Chapter 4 : The basic level

I will use this semantic of basic level so I can introduce the depth of trance which offers the most possibilities to manage pain. In the science of Hypnosis and in the Elmanian Hypnosis, there is a specificity against the Ericksonian Hypnosis in that we talk about **depth levels of trance**. To make it simple, we believe that like in diving, there are stages. Depending on this stage, we do not see the same thing and we do not live the same thing.

In these levels, we find that suggestions are **more easily assimilated** by our partners. Basically, if you want to see some kind of fishes during your dive, you will have to go deeper, not that you wouldn't have necessarily met any before that…but much less.

For our neophytes, this level is **our basic level** ; for practitioners, this is the **somnanbulism** level.

We can reach this level with a very easy technique from Dave Elman : **To Pretend.** Or to 'act like'.

In his book, Dave Elman explains that even children are able to use this method and as a doctor presented his own 7year old daughter in front of amazed staff, at her capacity to trance and handle the pain. She doesn't use anything else but the 'act like'.

This will help you to 'open the communication' with your subconsious. This latter in the sciences of Hypnosis, is considered as a 5 year old child. And the 'act like' if we were a cowboy or an indian is natural for a child. It is sufficient then to **give suggestions**, to go down to our basic level.

This technique is **accessible for everyone**, you just need to go into an imaginary game, and we know that imagination brings us into the long term memories, emotions and so in our subconscious.

We offer a simple tool to **enter into communication with our subconscious** and we are now going to spend one or two minutes to dive into this basic level.

- **Act as if** you were five years old, close your eyes and imagine that **you cannot open them again**, as a child would show you that he/she is trying to but can't. Do the test to see if you allow yourself this first.

For Practitioners : If your partner opens his/her eyes, your explanation was not clear enough or was not followed by your partner.

You can repeat the instructions and eventually put forward the deal of the beginning which is to go half way in order to have a positive result.

For Learners : If you open your eyes, ask yourself, do **you allow yourself in order to let go** so that you can reach this appeasing objective. The playful principle is an interesting key for the **letting go.**

- Now, you are going to **breathe in deeply** and at the end of this big inhalation you are going to open your eyes, then, **exhale deeply** and close your eyes when your lungs are completely empty. Repeat this three times minimum while saying '**I act as if I am doubling my relaxation state**'. The breathing permits you to really relax and appease yourself, to relax more and more.

For Practitioners : We are in a deepening stage called fractionation.

We allow, like in diving, to go back up in the stage so that we can go deeper each time.

For Learners : Look well within yourself this relaxation sensation, do not worry if you are not more relaxed, the most important is to '**Act as if**'/**to pretend'.**

Often I advise to **imagine yourself as the most relaxed possible** in order to invite your being to do what fits you most.

- Put your hand on your forehead and the other one behind your head where the occipital region is and as you would carry the head of a baby.

Close your eyes and count down from ten to one acting as if you are walking down a beautiful light source.

For Practitioners : In your practice, you can keep on with the classical deepenings from the Elman Induction until the transition for the mental relaxation.

For Learners : This technique is coming from Kinesiology and we find it back also in other systems like EMDR. It permits to relax the body and mind quickly, allowing you to go even deeper in Trance.

- The second part of this induction allows us to **continue to 'act as if'**. Imagine simply that you are going to count down from one hundred to one. Between each number, you are going to take the time to **double your connection state and relaxation** within your self. You are in the dynamic to 'act as if', which permits you to **suggest** yourself before the number 95, you will be well connected and ready to work on the different pains of your body.

For Practitioners : In practice, this part is more often used for the **mental relaxation**. In fact, it is at this moment that you will move from the **catalepsy level to the amnesic level**.

In the Elman Induction, the count down that you propose is orientated in one goal, the one which allows your partner to not count down out loud but to estimate that he/she arrived to **the stage you have chosen : the Somnanbulant level**.

For learners : this induction's facet is really useful and you need to **really look for doubling your state** between each number. This is important because to double your relaxation or connection state asks a **real implication and responsability** from yourself. For example, you can imagine the state you are in at the moment. You may be stressed, relaxed or pensive, whatever this state is, it is in level one. Now if I ask you to double the state you are in, you need to appreciate that **it asks an internal acknowledgement**. Therefore if you do this on at least 5 numbers, you really are going to feel that the '**act as if**' offers you the possibility to fully find yourself back. And if you don't succeed just yet, just carry on with more numbers and give yourself **the right to go to your basic level**.

Now, we have arrived in this basic level which permits us during our exercises to **answer in a simple and efficient way** to many **suggestions**.

You need to know that the suggestions that we use in hypnosis represent **some kind of program which we apply to ourselves**. It is interesting to note that with **different suggestions**, we can propose to our spirit to **intervene on our perception** of pain.

I will give you several exercises, please keep in mind that all humans are different and **do not answer to the same types of program**.

For Practitioners : Remember that depending on the different channel of communications, your partners will be **more or less** receptive to different suggestions.

When we are dealing with pain, we can be under the impression that the principal channel would be kinesthesic. It is important to know that in order to change perceptions we can **go through the other channels** which will influence the kinesthesic. Moreover, for some people, **dissociation** is possible through other communication channels. It allows **to separate ourself much more easily** from pain than to constantly try to diminish it.

For Learners : when we ask to understand suggestion as a program, we ask you to use the **principle of imagination**. Not everyone is good at it. In order to simplify, I will use the word **imagination**, but note that just the fact to think about or to 'act as if' will be enough to get noticeable results.

You can in all suggestions, ideas or propositions, **use different meaning**. You can be more visual, aural, kinesthesic, smell or taste sensitive…do not focus on what is the less easier for you.

Your reference is perception that you will have in your **basic level**. So, if you are more visual in your every day lifestyle, it is possible, that at this level, you feel **more easily** body or sound sensations.

It is also useful to remember that you are going to live your own way all suggestions made. There is no better way and if one exercise or suggestion doesn't fit or give any results (after 10 attempts), it just means that for this pain, it is not a good solution. **Respect your own ways to feel**. Do not pressure yourself, on the opposite, try to relax.

Chapter 5 : Technique of the Glove Anesthesia / Analgesia

This technique of the glove anesthesia is a **basic** in hypnosis. To try it, just follow these instructions :

- Go to your **basic level**
- Imagine your right hand being your left hand and vice versa, **plunge it into an iced bath of water**. Try to imagine, **by suggestion** that your hand becomes colder and colder and slowly, **reconnect** with these sensations which you have had of winter. Find back a memory where your hand was **very cold**, for example whilst skiing or walking outside in minus degree temperature.
- As you are going to connect to a memory of your body, your are at the same time going to **give information** to your brain, then to your hand to make it colder and colder. If you want, you could **extend this sensation to your whole arm.**
- Once the sensation is there, you succeed to engage with one of the capacities of your body, you succeed to **change its temperature**. You can start by **congratulating** your self for this first step. Now you are going to gently direct your hand to the top of your head.

There are two ways of doing this : either by imagining that helium baloons are under your arm and lift it up or by deliberately putting your hands in the chosen place.

- When your arm is on the top of your head, **continue to engage with this cold sensation** Then, you are going to focus on the other hand.

- On the second hand, you are going to create relaxation, try to relax it completely, it is **very simple to do**. Step by step, imagine that you **extend this relaxation to the rest of your body,** simply by **thought**. Trust yourself, imagine that it is diffusing. While continuing to imagine the relaxation through all your body, you are going to focus back on your hand, the one upon your head and you realise that it **loses sensibility**. It is as your **hand was numb**. You notice that the rest of your body relaxes more and more.

- When you are at this stage, after approximatively five minutes, you are going to put your hand onto the painful body part. As you are in your **basic level**, you are going to notice soon that it is very easy **to diffuse this analgesia sensation to the painful body part.**

Moreover, as you already have relaxed your body with your other hand, **diffusion towards other body parts will happen naturally.**

- If the painful part is not accessible with your hand, then you just need to put your **analgesised hand the closest** to the painful part and to **diffuse the sensation** to it.

You will see that this technique allows you to very quickly **diminish the pain** and that you can renew the experience regularly.

Lesser and lesser you will have to renew the whole process. You will be able to assign the analgesia in all your body parts **simply by thought and suggestion.** They will also be more precise and according to your needs.

For Practitioners : there would be two elements to look at. The first one is to **connect well your partner to the cold sensation** and the second is to allow the hand over the head **enough time** so that the blood circulating in it gives this sensation of tingling or torpor. Both hands are important even if more than often we use only one of them. Indeed, sometimes, the partner can focus so much on the hand over his head that he **may not stay tuned to himself.**

Dissociation, along with the diffused suggestion of relaxation in the whole body, gives to the subconscious the capacity to finish the work of analgesia and to prepare for the next step. Relaxation allows an **easier diffusion** of the suggestion and felt sensation of apeasement.

For learners : you have to take the time to **really feel the different variation** of sensation in your body. You focus on perceptions and as you are in your basic level, you can **let yourself be carried out.** It is through these sensations that you will be able to change completely sensations in your body, for example pain, and that you will be able to orientate this new way of feeling into your whole body.

To go further, you can also use the **metaphorical suggestion of a lake.** As the glove anesthesia, it is a basic in hypnosis. I would advise that you go to this next level when you **have learned to master** and that you can repeat easily and quickly the glove anesthesia.

The Lake's method helps your thoughts **into an imaginary perspective, visual people will find it particularly helpful.** You can put in it the whole of your beliefs and expectations that you have for yourself in these sessions. Imagination allows you to see new possibilities and offers **visualisation and a quicker assimilation of changes** we are looking for.

Moreover, it is very often used in sophrology, CBT or neurolinguistic programs. When at your **basic level**, you are simply going to start to imagine, counting down ten to one, that you are walking down a path leading to the lake. Once at the lake, you can imagine that you are **going into the lake** and that **progressively** you enter in it starting with your feet. You, then, have to be able to feel the **same sensations as the glove analgesia** and coming from your toes to the top of your head.

It is for you to suggest yourself this progressive rise of the coolness and numbness in your whole body. It is enough to imagine this sensation, you just have to **remember a memory from a dive into a pool or the sea**. It will permit you, in addition to the possibility of relieving your pain, to suggest to your subconscious **curative, progressive and positive suggestion**.

For Practitioners : this tool is really pertinent so that your partner can step by step realise the **possible global capacity** enhanced in trance and to alleviate, even retrieve pain. Take the time to know if your partner doesn't have any **phobia or traumatic event** linked to water. If it is the case, then you can try to go more toward the sensation of **heat than cold**. Indeed, depending on the pain and the perception of it, some sensibilities express themselves through a **cold sensation**.

In this case, I replace the lake by an old crater offering natural hot water springs. There is here this earth energy, a very primary energy which can really relax the body.

For Learners : It has to be nourished by your imagination. You are the one who, through your orientation, is giving **all the positives elements of this place.** Once created, it will be a reusable **resource** for you. Many partners, suffering from chronic pains, tell me that they were using this **under the shower** in the morning in order to have a more appeased day. Remember that you can go into your basic level whilst **being active**. It will get easier to enter into it and you will be able to use whilst walking, showering or even in transportation.

This first exercice is **really useful to understand your trance** but also to connect with yourself and to try the first **suggestions** with physiologic impact. We will see that some exercices will require the help of a practitioner, or a **good command** of this basic tool.

Once the Learner has understood his basic level and the impact of suggestion on the body, a large range of possibilities become available to apease daily life.

Chapter 6 : To communicate with your pain.

This exercice is as much **for beginners as experts**. It is true that the intervention of a practitioner can sometimes **help for a better decoding** of what represents pain. However, for the learners, you already have the capacity to **hear yourself better** through the good command you acquired during your basic level.

Pain is an information which can be put aside, even completely forgotten about so that suffering partners can **live better** lives.

Our psyche makes us attend to our pain in a different way, and especially for these chronic ones, when we consider that **the body is telling us about a facet of the subconscious**. Our subconscious didn't succeed to understand the information causing **somatisation,** like a loud alarm asking us a more particular attention. But the problem is that, by willing to **only reduce and forget the pain**, we forget about this alarm. Medicine which treats the pain in order to improve comfort **doesn't allow the body to express itself**. In other words and in this scenario, the subconscious tries to communicate with the conscious but **doesn't succeed**, then turns to the body which will not give a better answer if **we switch it off**.

Literally, we do not let him go through **comprehension, welcoming and acceptance** of the information/alarm.

Hypnosis can really help in this, to improve the communication. Whilst trying to communicate with pain, we **won't have a direct answer,** clear or precise. But we will comprehend slightly better what it is. We are going to realise that when we have peaks of pain, with who we have them, in which circumstances and a whole set of elements which will help us to see pain in a whole new way.

For most people with chronic pain, they know that **the level of it varies**. There are better and worse. Sometimes we understand that because we are tired, pain increases, or if we are stressed, upset. Everyone is different and pain from the same pathology will be experienced differently and at different time. Moreover, perception and pain management are very personal as it is all about understanding your own message to yourself. And the message can be different.

Practitioners will ask you **precise, continued and recurrent questions**. Often when the source of the pain is expressed, it reduces or even disappears. Without trying to make it disappear in the first place, we observe the effect on our body and listen to the different information of our being.

Firstly, you need to go to your **basic level**. Now that you can go there, you are going to **connect with your pain**. When I talk about connection, I mean that you are going to **focus on it.**

For people suffering from chronic pain, it may seem a **little more difficult**. Paradoxically, the fact that pain is constant makes it more difficult to **figure out the source** of the problem. Focus your spirit on the **origin** of pain. Where does it come from ? How does it develop ? Is it fuzzy ? Is it continuous ? Does it diffuse ? Is it only in one place ? Really take the time to **localise** it and to **not avoid its presence**. For some, the simple fact of welcoming pain without **repulsing** it, acknowledging it already offers a form of **relief**. The physical pain doesn't necessarily diminish but it is more precise, palpable. Once you have this link with your pain, you are going to try to **bring it somewhere else**. It is a **symbolic move** by thoughts. Just imagine a place, a peaceful one, a comfort zone.

The real work starts here. You are going to do a **basic questionning** about your pain. As you are in your basic level, it is interesting to note all answers whether **physiological, mental or emotional** you are going to receive. Learning how to listen to ourselves can be **surprising**. Depending upon your communication channels, you are going to get diverse information which can be visual, kinesthetic or otherwise.

Do not expect ready-made phrases or any precise elements. With experience, some of you, will really grasp the **capacity to hear yourselves**. Firstly, you just notice your thoughts and sensations for each question.

Often learners and partners will have this first answer : I don't know. How is everything going ? I advise you to **trust yourself**. You can put in front of you paper and pen to write down your feelings when a question is asked. Note the first words which come to your mind. Even let come to you all association. Connect to your pain and answer simple questions : **Who, what, when, how and why.** Pain can bring back into your mind someone in particular, maybe it will make no sense and appear completely incoherent, without any link to what you think your pain is. It is fine, we are trying to identify the who. When you connect to the pain, the person which comes to your mind will give **interesting indications** on the link : **pain > person.**
The question 'what' is interesting because it can really bring all sorts of images, words or thoughts. **Trust yourself**, even if it can seem weird, without any logic.

For Neophytes : it may not seem without interest. However, when we know that our subconscous is **constantly** trying to give us indications, we can admit that **no information given is without interest**. Then, if you think of something when connected to something else, that is because your spirit sees a **link** and that in this image, thought…there is a **clue, maybe an answer**. You will realise that all questions will bring you **essential information.**

It is in this discovery of perception that you will, step by step, and still connected to the pain, being conscious of the **different facets of yourself**.

For Practitioners : you are going to guide your partner with general questions at first, then more and more precise. Think of constantly reminding your partner to give you **a notation on their pain level**. You will then observe that according to the question, the pain can **increase**. It is a sign that we are touching an important **emotional or mental component**. For example : When you question the 'how', your partner goes **directly into regression** to the day he/she has been hurt. You are then going to question the whole of **his/her element of life** at this moment. Pain will give a **gauge** of the things to look into or not. You will be able to question your partner on his/her work, family, all of his/her life.

You will easily **make connections**. Maybe stress was high, maybe over a few months emotions were unstable or that the mental were going to negative thoughts. Once you have **identified** the different recurrent and important elements, ask him/her if the **pain increases or diminishes**. If you are on a high peak, focus a part of the session on this. The next step will be to find **direct suggestions** in sync with the problem discovered.

For Learners : Listen to your body. When you have some pain variation, you can note an important element to look into.

With **simple suggestions**, like : « I forgive myself », « I diminish more and more pain », «I am appeased ». You are going to be able to offer to your subconsious and your body real appeasement. As I noted before, this communication will bring answers as well, and positive and progressive suggestions are really useful options in order to listen to yourself.

Chapter 7 : Work associated to the pain (Only for Practitioners).

In the previous chapter, I talked about a **dialogue principle**, I would like to put forward a technique which gives **impressive results**. Please note, to do so, this means you bring your partner into a **very painful state**.

This method uses two elements.

The first one is the **regression to the trauma,** at the exact moment when the pain has been the highest. The body has a memory, the subconscious will use this memory as an **indicator to the information** which is given. You need to tell your partner that the level of pain will increase **exponentially** during this phase.

The second is the **association**. We know that, generally speaking, in hypnosis, we are in **dissociative techniques** when referring to pain time, there is no dissociation, on the opposite, we are **going to increase the pain to its paroxysm.**

Let's understand how it works. **Pain is a communication** so when it is high, that means that the **alarm given is important**. The more the pain is high, then the more the communication about it is **imperative to catch our attention**.

We are going to make our partner go back to **the highest point of this communication**, most of the time, it is the moment of the trauma. We will be in the **association of pain and trance** in order to interrogate the partner emotionally, physically and mentally.

All **information** given, **memories, values** transmitted with the pain or **beliefs on pain,** its management and representation, will give us plenty of indication to understand better and link things. Moreover, this **capacity of the human being** to go back to a high level of pain, opens the **almost instant possibility to make it lower.** It is **like a teaching to the subconscious** and the body, which, with simple suggestion and a simple connection to a memory, will make it possible to slow down the intensity of pain. Let's look at an example : Our partner tells us that he is twelve over ten whilst within his high peak. Normally, at the beginning of the technique, he is around five.

In less than five minutes, we have made the body take this intensity of pain. This, only by **suggestion and emotional connection.** We teach the body **this capacity to be flexible** on pain. Once we have the information needed to continue the session, we are going to make the pain decrease and, surprisingly, most of the time we will go back to a lower notation of pain than at the beginning.

In our example, our partner goes down at three

- Firstly, ask your partner the level of his/her pain between **one and ten**.
- Bring him/her to the **somnambulant level.**
- Ask him/her to focus on the pain of his body he wants to work on and **connect** him/her fully to the pain. Suggestions will help orientate this connection.
- Give him/her a suggestion type : « we are going to go back to the source of your pain connecting it with the trauma of your body and spirit. ».
- The partner is going to say that the pain increases, you will need to accompany him and start to **interrogate on the set of perceptions,** sensations, emotions and all different ideas which come to his/her mind.

Pain is often linked with a set of events, emotions. When your partner will be in a **trance of pain,** all the information that he will give to you, and there will be a lot, will permit you to **go back to important sources.**

It is probable that your partner doesn't go back necessarly to the accident or to the first pain felt. Even if **the images do not correspond** and even if they are incoherent, treat them as if they were the **real key point of the session.**

Sometimes we say that **pain can make one delirious**. This is the exact delirium that we will use, the subconscious allowing itself to give a lot of information at this moment.

As practitioners, it will be easy to **keep in mind the whole process** and to make it slow down through **peaceful suggestions** for pain. The descent has also its importance, beside the fact that it is an opportunity for our partner to manage his/her pain. Indeed to each level down in the countdown means that you can **interrogate more and more precisely** on what has been said before. The subconscious during peaks of pain will offer plenty of indications and the descent will permit us to **complete**, even understand better the way to express this pain.

With **direct suggestions of appeasement,** you are going to be able to slow down to the lowest level of pain. It is **more simple** than if we had started at the initial level of the pain. From this lower level, you can **start the session** on the multiple messages given during the process. Often a **simple expression** allows a real change in our partner. This facet of the work, which is to crop and manage the memory or the perception of it, opens a **deeper path** in the expression of the pain. You will realise then, that everything said will **conduct to other issues**, often far from the pain, at least in appearance. Links can be **surprising,** for the partner and for the practitioner.

To summarize, increase the pain to understand its different messages through the VAKOG, then make it slow down while continuing to interrogate the body and spirit in order to arrive to an acceptable level and lower. Finally, you will direct the session on what you have been given and following what is hidden behind.

Chapter 8 : Utilise the basic level as a source of change

We saw in the previous chapter tools allowing us to go back to the **source of the pain.** In this chapter, we are going to use the **basic level**. As I mentioned at the beginning of this book, the somnanbulant level is used in the Elmanian hypnosis as **level of reference** in order to diminish pain with simple suggestions. With this tool, we are not looking for causes, we are more into the symptomatic. The symptomatic is a **mandatory phase** in order to treat people in pain. We are not going to leave our partner in pain just to go back to the cause. Since the basic level, conscious and subconscious are in a **balanced trance**. This means that suggestions, conscious to subconscious, have a high probability to **give direct results.**

I only share this technique now because I estimate that you have repeated a **number of times** through previous instruction, which means that you have a good command of this somnanbulant level. Your basic level.

For Practitioners : if you apply the Elman induction, you will arrive with no doubt into the somnanbulant level. You still can check the different levels for example by testing a catalepsy, an amnesia and then a direct suggestion to appease the pain.

In this trance level, your partner is **able to talk** and so to give you easily his/her level of pain on a scale of one to ten. I would advise that you **make your partner talk all the way through the session**. You will give suggestions, **direct or metaphoric**, but avoid long talks and other tools which could bring confusion. The goal is to **infuse suggestions** in the subconscious and by extension in the body in order to get a complete return on what has been proposed. You can for example, ask for the pain to disappear using coolness. **The return of your partner will be essential** and in order to continue and progress in the suggestions you make. If your partner didn't feel any better with the coolness, try the warmth. If the warmth doesn't work, propose a distanciation and so on, **stay flexible.**

It is essential that at each suggestion, **you repeat at least three times,** you also make your partner repeat these out loud or quietly. Also that you ask him his return on his scale of one to ten. Once you have succeeded to make the pain go down, which is usually **quick** until a certain level, check already that this new level of pain is **more agreeable than the previous** one, and ask if it has been a long time since the appeasement started. You can make your partner **aware of his capacity of pain management** and already **anchor this level**, even if it is not the level zero.

So many people suffering from chronic pain are so satisfied to be able to go lower than the level five that they will have **great satisfaction**.

It is important that you realise that pain gives also **secondary benefits**. Some people are **not ready to quit a habit** which they lived with for so many years.

Pain is a habit, it is important also for its set of positive things. If you lower it too quickly, the expression of the pain is not respected anymore, you take the risk that the expression of the pain will reappear higher and somewhere else.

An advice for people who have pain gravitating around eight, nine or ten…make them go not lower than four or five. First, you give them the right **to have kept this pain during all these years** and the possibility to **not feel guilty** when, and sometimes in one session, pain can disappear completely. It is not nothing. Imagine a person **who realises that he/she kept the pain for years when it could have been dealt with in less than an hour.** Practitioners want often to do better than good and do not see the impact of a change so important. You can also show to your partner that suggestions work and that **with the activation of an anchor,** he/she can, with work, diminish or reduce pain. Going too fast, you risk to create an auto sabotage in your partner.

It is important to keep in mind that we **can't take the whole pain** away but diminish it at its maximum.

Indeed, pain is an information and doctors do not estimate that it doesn't have any interest at all…to bring it down at **level one or two is sufficient**. As practitioners, your **suggestions will step by step, level down** the pain.

I would advise that you put an anchor at the lower level and different from the previous. This method is symptomatic and **works really well**. You can, if you want to, in the second phase, work on the **origin of the pain**. Most of the time, your partners will be satisfied and will **not want to go further** in their therapy. I remember one time, a partner of 70 years old came to see me. He was curved and had pains since he was 35 years old. He was an ex athlete and his chronic pains were affecting his ability to live properly. After one session, he went away with his spine much more straight and without any pain. The next session, when I asked him about the goal of the second session, he talks to me about something else than his pain which lasted more than 30 years. When I tell him that maybe it would be interesting to see what was behind the pain, he smiled and prefered to orientate his goal on something else. After this session, I never saw him again. It is normal that someone who had strong pain does not necessarily want to work on the **psychological aspect of it**.

The only thing that I can warn with my previous experience is that regularly, **pain can come back somewhere else** to be understood.

For Learners : You need to go to your **basic level** and then make **direct suggestions**. The latter are composed as the following : They are **short, positive and progressive**. For example : « My pain diminishes as I take deep long breathes in ». You can work on **one suggestion**, rather direct, or **a series of suggestions** of the same type. The second way to do suggestions is quite **metaphoric**. For example : « I imagine step by step that I go down alongside a valley. As I walk down the path, I feel my body more and more light, my respiration is deeper and I feel better and better. I arrive near a lake. I take my time before immersing myself into the lake and at each breath I imagine the coolness from top to toe appease my whole body… » I will come back to **the lake** in this essay, it is a technique that really works well.

I also propose the **tree of possibilities** which is an interesting metaphor for the pain management, and which all learners can assimilate and apply quickly in order to appease.

Types of direct suggestion are really **what I advise** the most, for the practitioners and for the learners.

The only necessary thing to have is the basic level, the somnanbulant level. Once you get there, **suggestions function** quickly and results are easy. If you are used to direct hypnosis, as it is the case in **the science of hypnosis**, you **can also use some hypnotic phenomenon** in order to allow suggestion to give a quick return to your partners.

For example, work on a **cataleptic phenomenon for an arm which can't bend** or alternatively, is completely weak.

You know that where there is this phenomenon, it is easy to make a **suggestion** that the arm is **an iron bar or better, that this arm which became a bar doesn't have any sensibility**. As there is no more sensibility, pain can't be there. Once you have tested on a part of your arm that the **phenomenon analgesia hypnosis is there**, you just need to **make a suggestion to generalise** this sensation throughout the whole body. This way has a big advantage, it is that already during the test, your partner **observes already the diminishing of the sensation of pain** in the arm.

Generalisation in the whole body can then happen very quickly and offering, through the process, a way to **repeat the process and to give back autonomy to your partner**. Hypnotic phenomenon are rarely used in practice, we lend them more often to the urban scene, which is a shame.

It would be a very **powerful lever**, an **immediate proof** of the capacity to reduce pain, even to remove it completely in a few seconds. We could call this a form of persuasion, allowing the **quick assimilation of suggestions and physiologic returns** of this technique.

To summarise :

- Put your partner in trance directed to the basic level
- Stretch the arm and suggest : « The arm is going to be more and more rigid, more and more solid as the most solid of iron bars, once it is only an iron bar, not only this, I can't bend it. »
- Once you have verified that the phenomenon works, there is no need to be 100% efficient, a simple resistance indicates already that the suggestion works. You are going to go to the next suggestion
- Remember to ask your partner where he/she is on a scale of one to ten.
- The arm is an iron bar, an iron bar without any sensation of pain, just a bar, no sensation….
- Think again to ask about the scale
- Once verified, that the arm is less sensitive and with less pain, go to the next suggestion

- « This neutral and appeased sensation generalises itself and step by step is going from the arm to the back etc. »

Chapter 9 : Therapy Pretest (TPT) as a progressive tool to appease

As seen previously, we can use **hypnotic phenomenon to appease pain**. For practitioners and learners who already know the principle of the pretest, I have developed a **whole system** around this **basic phenomenon**, which works with everyone.

We can use it, like most of techniques in this context, by working directly on the **symptom**, or under the **form of a dialogue** as we have seen before. To define what I call pretest and that we work with a common definition, this tool is the **use of the ideomotor answer** of the partner's arm. To make them answer to a suggestion of lightness – heaviness or attraction – repulsion. This phenomenon is particularly interesting as it gives us a **direct return** from the dialogue and the orientation proposed to subconscious.

In our goal of **pain management**, it offers us the capacity to propose to subconscious an indication, through suggestion, and to see the result through the **physiological return**, for example the arms which attract each other (if this command has a real impact to the goal we want to achieve)

For Practitioners : You are going to ask your partner to give a **notation** on the scale for their pain. Then **with or without induction**, the **questioning** work already seen before and the TPT **open automatically the trance**.

- Make your partner stretch his arm, one palm up and the other palm directed down.
- Put into the palm up the **weight of the pain** and in the other the **will** to get out of it.
- Explain that the will is going to make the hands go up and that the weight is going to bring the other one down.

This first step is interesting as to see what the **subconscious gives information** like with regards to the pain. Some people give notations of seven or eight but then when you ask them to imagine their pain, in weight, volume or form…you can see that the **answer from the subconscious is not as strong** than the one expressed by the conscious.

It can be disturbing and it is important to **ask questions about it to your partner** as to his/her perception of the pain. Indeed, if the subconscious determines that the weight of the pain is not so heavy, it is maybe because **something else is weighing in**. In this case, I advise to look for **secondary benefits** that your partner put in place in his/her everyday life.

As explained previously, there are chances that consciously **he/she doesn't accept the idea that there are benefits of pain.** This will be part of the complete session and, in this case, you are not going to touch **directly** the pain but the **cause** of the pain. On the other side, if the hand with the suggestion of elevation according to **motivation doesn't go up or very little**, there is no question to ask. Maybe the **motivation to appease the pain** is not as strong as the one expressed. Keep in mind that **your partner doesn't lie** but that **he is not listening to his/her subconscious.** Indeed, you can see that the pain was one of the expressions that he/she never recognised and that the scubconscious, when asked directly, **doesn't give answers which match what the mental state proposes.**

The interest of the PTT is that your partner cannot **deny the movements of his/her** ams and then can be aware of **the dichotomy existing in him/her.**

You are going to have different scenarios and depending on these, you will have to adapt the session according to the results of the pretest.

Either you go for a therapy which **will not be based on the pain management**, at least not for this session. Or you orientate towards the pain management, keeping in mind that it is not necessarily the real issue. Let me remind you that pretest allows us to see aswell how the partner reacts and so to adapt **more**

easily the semantic which will fit him/her best. The following tool is very easy and will allow you to diminish the pain of your partner, making him aware of potential resistance by having an **open discussion** with him/her.

- Put his/her two hands in the front and place them together
- Explain the idea that one side is the body and the other one pain
- You are going to separate the two hands through **suggestions allowing to create distance between the body and the pain.**

This exercise works **quickly and easily**. You can see all the resistance that your partner puts in place, some will even have what we call **reactance**, which mean a reaction **against** the fact that it might work. If it is the case, you need to go back to some work on the **secondary benefits**.

For Leaners : You can use the '**Act as if**' with your basic level. If you never have been hypnotised and that you never have done a pretest, it is fine.

You are going to simply take the second part of what is proposed to the practitioners.

- **Put your hands together,** arms strecthed and focusing in order to put all your pain in the right hand and in the other one the sensation of well being you want to go to.
- Act as if the two hands were repulsing each other. In this exercise, **your imagination will lead the work**, with a suggestion like : « as my hands repulse each other, pain diminish, the pain is going away ».

Your **concentration put in this exercise to imagine the force** wich push away your hands will become the factor releasing your well being. **Trust yourself,** this phenomenon is very simple and at your basic level you can do it ! You can repeat it a few times and you will learn how to manage pain with this exercise of the pretest.

Conclusion

Here are **some techniques** that you will easily put in place as a practitioners or partners. Before to go to other techniques, I would advise that you **work on these basic ones** I already shared which will give you many possibilities.

My goal is not to give an long list of preocesses but more to **create awareness of the different principles** which can emerge from hypnosis and regarding the pain management.

In a few months, i will propose another book, with other techniques. Before that, **take the time to work and practice** these ones.

Like for videos, I want **interactivity.** If you have any questions, remarques or if you want more informations, send me an email **(hype.ose@gmail.com)** and I will answer to it in my next book.

You can easily, under hypnosis, solve many issues even if it has been years and that it looks insuperable.

Subconscious and unconscious offer a **perception of the reality**. It is up to you to **change this reality** and to apease more and more body pain.

Take care of yourself.
Be One
Pank (July 2015)

Who is Christophe Pank ?

I'm French man from Paris. I've worked in hypnosis, Npl, personal development and energic healing, since i'm teen. I share my experience and knowledge everyday and i created HnO (Hype-N-Ose) Hypnose in 2010, to help people to learn about themselves and psycho-pratictionner to increase their knowledge.

Now, i want share with you my ideas with essays, videos, audios. I know more we open our mind to different way of thinking and more we develop our own special capacity to become what we are, really.

Take time to watch my english Youtube Channel : hnohypnosis and my website : www.hnohypnosis.com.

You have a such big potential in you, you can open your door and go on the field of your life.

www.ingramcontent.com/pod-product-compliance
Lightning Source LLC
Chambersburg PA
CBHW050757240726
48654CB00008B/519